First English-language edition published 1986 in the U.K. by
Hodder and Stoughton
This U.S. edition published 1986 by Derrydale Books, distributed
by Crown Publishers, Inc.

Library of Congress Cataloging-in-Publication Data

Scarry, Huck.
   Things that fly.

   Translation of: Lo sai come si vola?
   Summary: Traces the history and explains the
scientific principles of flight.
   1. Flight — Juvenile literature.   [1. Flight]
I. Title
TL547.S33513   1986   629.13   85-29352
ISBN 0-517-61657-2

h g f e d c b a

Printed in Spain by Artes Gràficas Toledo S.A.
D. L. TO:330-1986

Huck Scarry

Things that Fly

Derrydale Books
New York

The Ocean of Air

Air is all around us. Whichever way we turn, and reaching high above our heads, there is air. The entire Earth is surrounded by a sphere of air, called the atmosphere, so vast and deep that it is sometimes nicknamed the Ocean of Air.

Mount Everest
the highest point on Earth
29,028 ft (8,848 m)

Mont Blanc
the highest point in the Alps
15,771 ft (4,807 m)

9,000 m

8,000 m

7,000 m

6,000 m

5,000 m

4,000 m

3,000 m

2,000 m

1,000 meters

Sea level

Eiffel Tower, Paris
1,050 ft (320 m)

Modern jet airliners cruise
at altitudes in the region
of 20,000–40,000 ft (6,000–12,000 m).

Sea level

Sea level

1,000 meters

2,000 m

3,000 m

In 1963 the American experimental rocket aircraft X-15 reached over 350,650 ft (107,000 m), well into space!

The stratosphere lies above the troposphere. Modern jet aircraft fly in this less dense layer of the atmosphere.

The U-2 spy plane could fly at about 65,500 ft (20,000 m).

In 1935 the American balloon Explorer II, piloted by Captain Anderson and Captain Stevens, rose to over 72,000 ft (22,000 m).

Professor Piccard was the first man to reach the stratosphere. In 1932 his balloon, the FNRS, rose to over 52,500 ft (16,000 m).

∧
Stratosphere
Troposphere
∨

22,000 m
21,000 m
20,000 m
19,000 m
18,000 m
17,000 m
16,000 m
15,000 m
14,000 m
13,000 m
12,000 m
11,000 m
10,000 m
9,000 m
8,000 m
7,000 m
6,000 m
5,000 m
4,000 m
3,000 m

Concorde can cruise at altitudes of up to over 62,000 ft (19,000 m).

5,000 m
6,000 m
7,000 m
8,000 m
9,000 m
10,000 m
11,000 m
12,000 m

Like the oceans on Earth, the Ocean of Air gets denser the deeper you go. We live at the bottom of the atmosphere, in its densest layer, called the troposphere. It is in the troposphere that weather occurs. We walk at the bottom of the Ocean of Air, like the crabs that crawl on the sea bed. Birds, balloons and airplanes fly through the air with the same ease as fish swim in the sea. How do they fly? It is, above all, thanks to the Ocean of Air itself that flight through it is possible.

When the Wind Blows

We are all held to the Earth by gravity. So, too, is the atmosphere. The Ocean of Air is made up of myriads of minute particles, or molecules, of air, just as the seas are made up of drops of water.

One drop of water weighs next to nothing, but how heavy a full bucket can be! In the same way, air particles can exert quite a force. The water of a river, rushing downstream, can carry boats, leaves and branches on its back. It is strong enough to turn water wheels.

Moving air can be powerful, too. A stiff breeze carries leaves on its back, blows smoke across the sky, tugs at the wash and the flags, snatches hats and scarves, sets toy pinwheels spinning. A strong wind turns great windmills, propels sailboats . . . and delights all fliers of kites!

Before steam engines and gasoline powered engines were invented, and before electricity was harnessed and put to practical use, the wind was one of the few sources of energy available. For thousands of years it has been turning windmills and pushing sailing ships around the world.

Lighter Than Air

Have you ever watched smoke rise from a fire? It seems to be lighter than air as it rises into the sky. Heat has an interesting effect on air. It excites it, making the particles move about furiously. Because each particle then needs more space to move in, the effect is to expand the air.

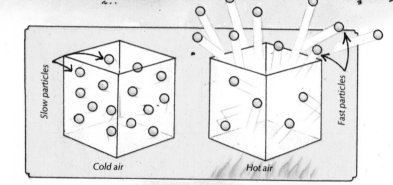

Slow particles

Fast particles

Cold air

Hot air

As there are fewer particles in hot air than cold air, hot air really does become lighter than cold. Smoke and ashes do indeed ride a hot wind skyward through a sea of cooler, heavier air.

Two hundred years ago, two brothers living in France, Joseph Michel and Jacques Etienne Montgolfier, were puzzled by smoke's ability to rise. They wondered if it would be possible to use rising smoke to lift something. They held a light, silken bag over a fire and watched it fill with smoke. After a while, it billowed, and tugged . . . lifting like magic into the air!

Encouraged by the success of their first experiments at home, the Montgolfier brothers made a big, spherical bag with sections of paper and cloth held together by buttons. They sent this balloon aloft in their home town of Annonay on June 5, 1783. The magical sight of the balloon defying gravity not only amazed the witnesses but also excited the curiosity of the whole world. It marked the beginning of the history of flight.

Balloons filled with hydrogen or helium gas (both are lighter than air) rise through the atmosphere as easily as bubbles through water.

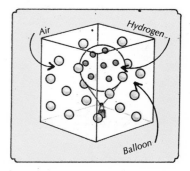

At a fair you can sometimes buy toy balloons. They are not filled with hot air but with a gas (usually helium) whose particles weigh less than those of the air. The balloons will escape from you quickly if you don't hold the string tightly.

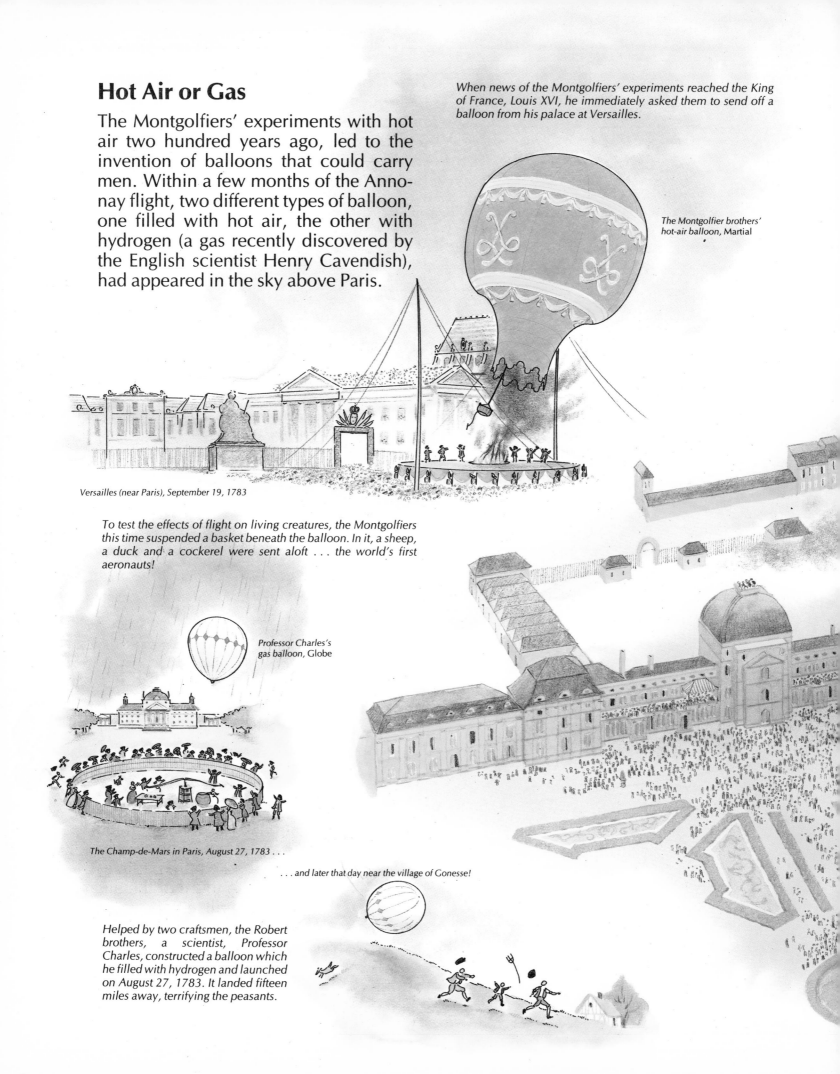

Hot Air or Gas

The Montgolfiers' experiments with hot air two hundred years ago, led to the invention of balloons that could carry men. Within a few months of the Annonay flight, two different types of balloon, one filled with hot air, the other with hydrogen (a gas recently discovered by the English scientist Henry Cavendish), had appeared in the sky above Paris.

When news of the Montgolfiers' experiments reached the King of France, Louis XVI, he immediately asked them to send off a balloon from his palace at Versailles.

The Montgolfier brothers' hot-air balloon, Martial

Versailles (near Paris), September 19, 1783

To test the effects of flight on living creatures, the Montgolfiers this time suspended a basket beneath the balloon. In it, a sheep, a duck and a cockerel were sent aloft . . . the world's first aeronauts!

Professor Charles's gas balloon, Globe

The Champ-de-Mars in Paris, August 27, 1783 . . .

. . . and later that day near the village of Gonesse!

Helped by two craftsmen, the Robert brothers, a scientist, Professor Charles, constructed a balloon which he filled with hydrogen and launched on August 27, 1783. It landed fifteen miles away, terrifying the peasants.

Flight over Paris in the Montgolfière balloon, November 21, 1783

Two months after the animal aeronauts had been brought down safely, two brave men, François Pilâtre de Rozier and the Marquis d'Arlandes, made a daring flight over the rooftops of Paris in the biggest balloon the Montgolfiers had yet built. Ten days later, Jacques Charles and Noël Robert ascended in a gas-filled balloon from the Tuileries gardens in Paris before an enormous crowd.

Pilâtre de Rozier and d'Arlandes had to stoke the fire burning at the mouth of the balloon.

Flight from the Tuileries gardens in the Charlière balloon, December 1, 1783

The hydrogen balloon carried Jacques Charles and Noël Robert twenty-seven miles from the French capital. The gas-filled Charlière was much easier to fly, and stayed aloft longer, than the hot-air Montgolfière.

Ballooning

A balloon is at the mercy of the winds and the weather, and piloting it skillfully is largely a matter of balancing the craft against air currents and weather conditions. Because hydrogen gas has a greater lifting power than the same volume of hot air, the envelope of a hot-air balloon (red and yellow stripes in the illustrations) must be much bigger than that of a gas-filled balloon (pink and white stripes).

As the balloons travel higher, so the surrounding atmosphere becomes less dense, and there is less outside pressure to hold the balloons in the air.

The more the air in a hot-air balloon is heated, the lighter it gets and the higher the balloon rises.

Throwing out ballast lightens a gas balloon and allows it to rise higher.

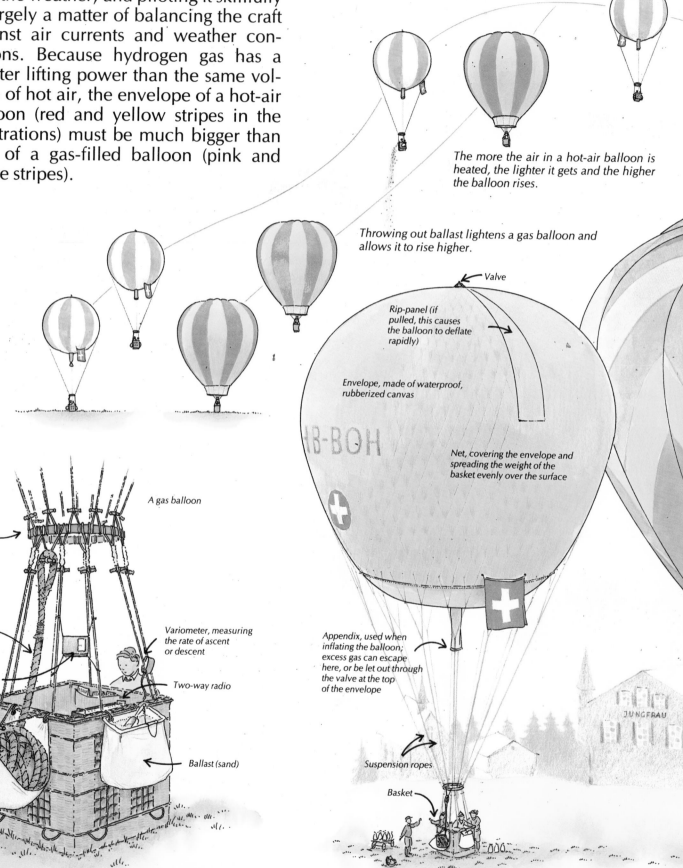

A gas balloon

Suspension hoop

Trailrope

Barometer, indicating altitude

Basket (of wicker, which absorbs shock)

Bags of ballast

Variometer, measuring the rate of ascent or descent

Two-way radio

Ballast (sand)

Valve

Rip-panel (if pulled, this causes the balloon to deflate rapidly)

Envelope, made of waterproof, rubberized canvas

Net, covering the envelope and spreading the weight of the basket evenly over the surface

HB-BOH

Appendix, used when inflating the balloon; excess gas can escape here, or be let out through the valve at the top of the envelope

Suspension ropes

Basket

JUNGFRAU

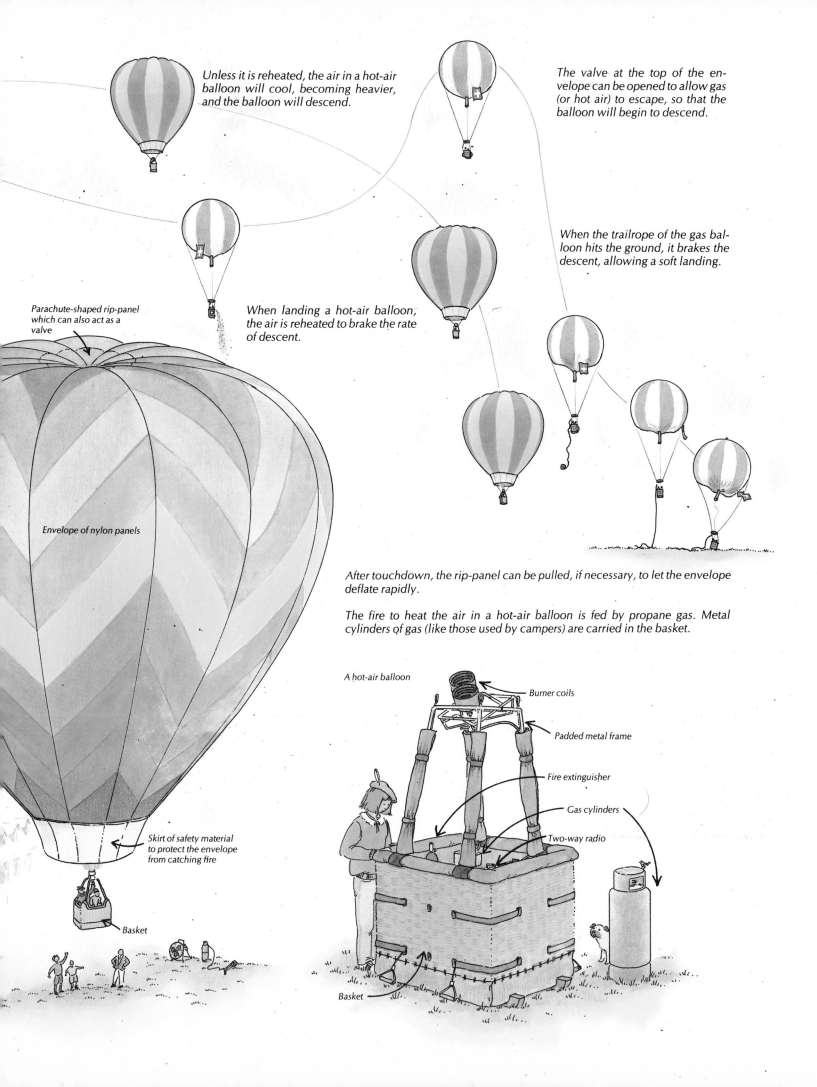

Unless it is reheated, the air in a hot-air balloon will cool, becoming heavier, and the balloon will descend.

The valve at the top of the envelope can be opened to allow gas (or hot air) to escape, so that the balloon will begin to descend.

When the trailrope of the gas balloon hits the ground, it brakes the descent, allowing a soft landing.

Parachute-shaped rip-panel which can also act as a valve

When landing a hot-air balloon, the air is reheated to brake the rate of descent.

Envelope of nylon panels

After touchdown, the rip-panel can be pulled, if necessary, to let the envelope deflate rapidly.

The fire to heat the air in a hot-air balloon is fed by propane gas. Metal cylinders of gas (like those used by campers) are carried in the basket.

A hot-air balloon

Burner coils

Padded metal frame

Fire extinguisher

Gas cylinders

Two-way radio

Skirt of safety material to protect the envelope from catching fire

Basket

Basket

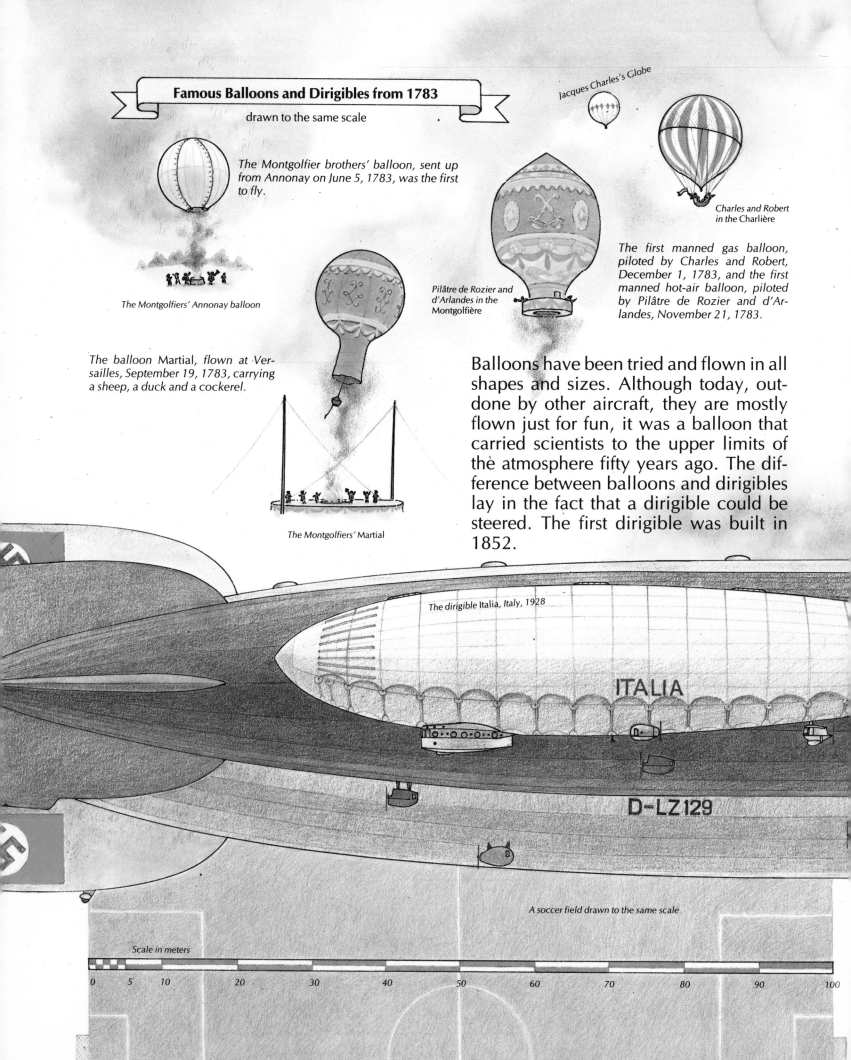

Famous Balloons and Dirigibles from 1783

drawn to the same scale

The Montgolfier brothers' balloon, sent up from Annonay on June 5, 1783, was the first to fly.

The Montgolfiers' Annonay balloon

The balloon Martial, flown at Versailles, September 19, 1783, carrying a sheep, a duck and a cockerel.

The Montgolfiers' Martial

Jacques Charles's Globe

Charles and Robert in the Charlière

The first manned gas balloon, piloted by Charles and Robert, December 1, 1783, and the first manned hot-air balloon, piloted by Pilâtre de Rozier and d'Arlandes, November 21, 1783.

Pilâtre de Rozier and d'Arlandes in the Montgolfière

Balloons have been tried and flown in all shapes and sizes. Although today, outdone by other aircraft, they are mostly flown just for fun, it was a balloon that carried scientists to the upper limits of the atmosphere fifty years ago. The difference between balloons and dirigibles lay in the fact that a dirigible could be steered. The first dirigible was built in 1852.

The dirigible Italia, Italy, 1928

ITALIA

D-LZ129

A soccer field drawn to the same scale

Scale in meters

| 0 | 5 | 10 | 20 | 30 | 40 | 50 | 60 | 70 | 80 | 90 | 100 |

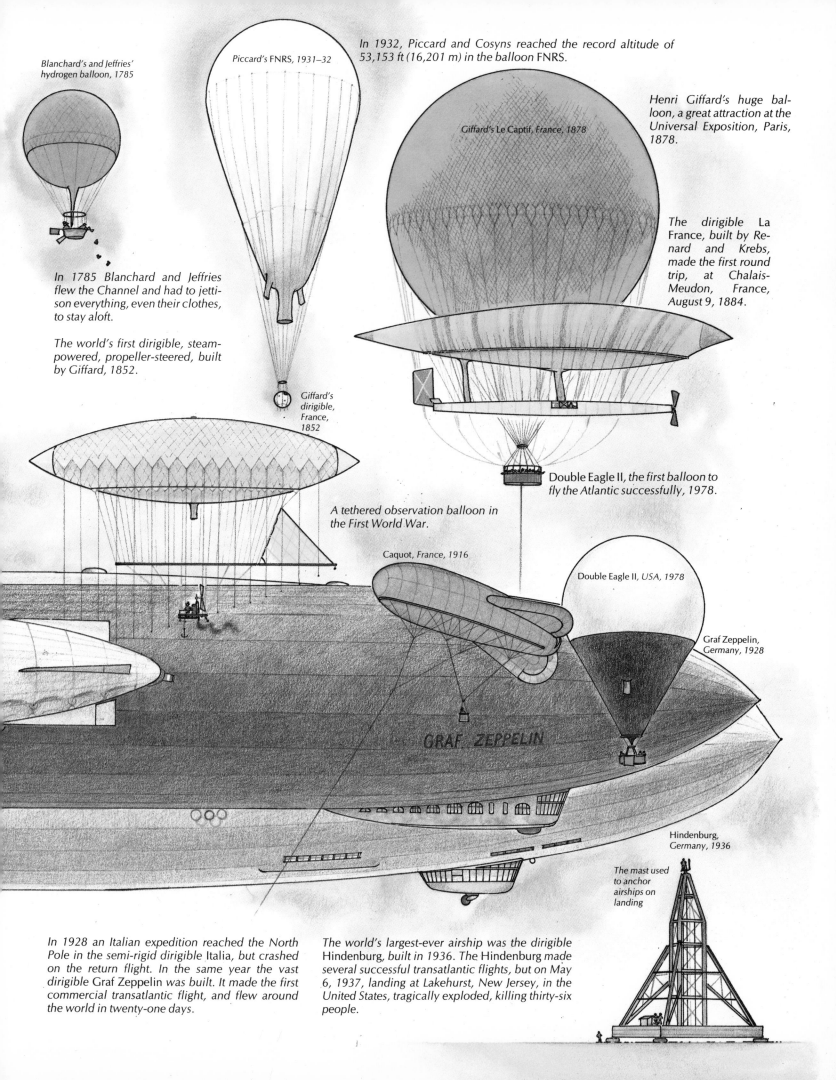

Blanchard's and Jeffries' hydrogen balloon, 1785

Piccard's FNRS, 1931–32

In 1932, Piccard and Cosyns reached the record altitude of 53,153 ft (16,201 m) in the balloon FNRS.

Henri Giffard's huge balloon, a great attraction at the Universal Exposition, Paris, 1878.

Giffard's Le Captif, France, 1878

In 1785 Blanchard and Jeffries flew the Channel and had to jettison everything, even their clothes, to stay aloft.

The world's first dirigible, steam-powered, propeller-steered, built by Giffard, 1852.

Giffard's dirigible, France, 1852

The dirigible La France, built by Renard and Krebs, made the first round trip, at Chalais-Meudon, France, August 9, 1884.

A tethered observation balloon in the First World War.

Caquot, France, 1916

Double Eagle II, the first balloon to fly the Atlantic successfully, 1978.

Double Eagle II, USA, 1978

Graf Zeppelin, Germany, 1928

GRAF ZEPPELIN

Hindenburg, Germany, 1936

The mast used to anchor airships on landing

In 1928 an Italian expedition reached the North Pole in the semi-rigid dirigible Italia, but crashed on the return flight. In the same year the vast dirigible Graf Zeppelin was built. It made the first commercial transatlantic flight, and flew around the world in twenty-one days.

The world's largest-ever airship was the dirigible Hindenburg, built in 1936. The Hindenburg made several successful transatlantic flights, but on May 6, 1937, landing at Lakehurst, New Jersey, in the United States, tragically exploded, killing thirty-six people.

Heavier Than Air

Unlike balloons, which are lighter than air, most things that fly are heavier than air. How do they do it? While apples plummet with a thud, autumn leaves slide gently to the ground. They are thin and flat, and ride on the back of the air particles beneath them. Leaves, kites and parachutes, all fly in this way.

Although the Italian artist Leonardo da Vinci drew designs for a parachute nearly five hundred years ago, the first man to put the idea into practice was André Jacques Garnerin.

Garnerin attached his parachute to the basket of a balloon, and on October 22, 1797, at a height of 1,000 meters above Paris, cut the suspension ropes and used the parachute to make a safe landing.

Drawing by Leonardo da Vinci, 1514

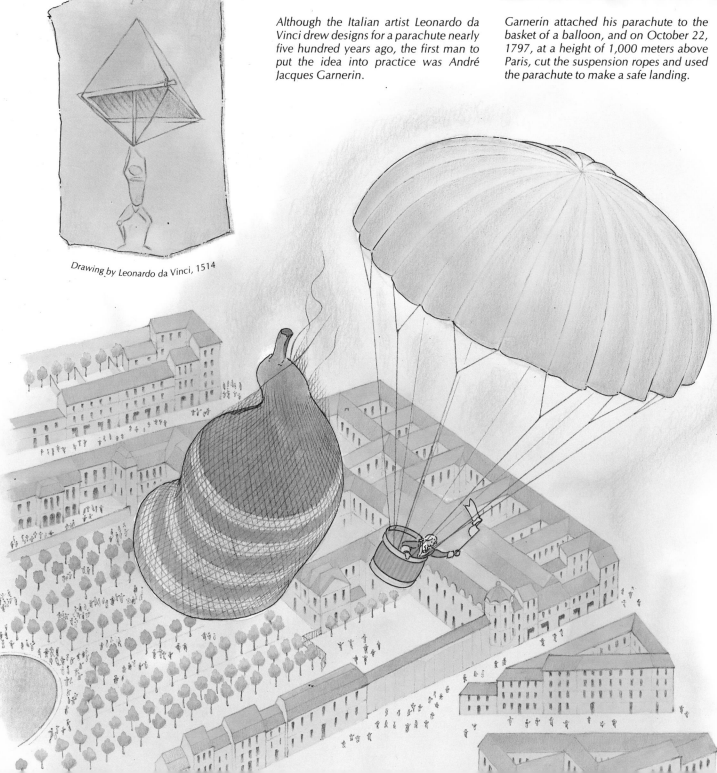

A parachute glides to earth in much the same way as a fallen leaf. Its broad canopy rests on the air as if on a cushion, using the air's resistance to soften the fall. Spacecraft returning to Earth use parachutes, and Concorde uses one as a brake when landing.

The atmosphere is made up of myriads of particles, which resist anything passing through the air. You can feel this resistance when you ride a bicycle, for instance. Given the right shape, an object can glide through the air, catching the air particles beneath it and sliding over them.

Drop a flat sheet of paper, and it will glide down through the air. Crumple it so that it cannot catch the air particles beneath it, and it falls straight to the ground. Toss a crumpled sheet of paper into the air, and it arches to the earth. Fold it properly, and it glides like a bird!

Birds

To glide earthward through the air is one thing. To propel yourself masterfully through it is quite another! Birds are nature's ultimate flying-machines. A good many insects are also able to fly. Of course, it is the bird's wings that enable it to fly. But wings alone are not enough.

Every part of a bird is adapted to flying. Its wings are aerodynamically shaped. Pushing against the air's resistance with a powerful downstroke of the wing moves the bird forwards. As it lifts its wings again, the outer feathers separate so that there is minimum resistance during the upstroke. At full upstroke they fold into a broad, smooth sweep of wing, ready for another powerful thrust downward. Different types of wing suit different styles of flight. A seagull has long, slim wings to glide swiftly over the water; a buzzard's broad wings and tail mean it can circle while waiting to swoop; the swallow has narrow wings to dart about rapidly, close to the ground, in search of insects; and the pheasant's short, wide wings enable it to flap quickly upward out of the undergrowth.

A bird's body is covered with feathers. There are different types for different functions. Soft downy feathers trap the air and keep the bird warm. Vaned feathers on the wings and tail are firm and sleek, and help the bird to fly and to steer.

Ear (covered by feathers)
Nape
Crown
Forehead
Back
Eye
Beak
Rump
Breast
Upper tail coverts
False knee
Tarsus
Rear toe
Under tail coverts
Jay

Semiplume
Vaned feather
Vaned feather with aftershaft
Filoplume (shaft with downy tip)
Rachis
Vane
Rachis
Quill
Barbules
Barb
Down

The close-up shows that the vanes are made up of barbs. Each barb is a miniature feather, with hundreds of barbules equipped with tiny hooks which latch on to the neighboring barbs.

Seagull

Buzzard

Swallow

Pheasant

During the upstroke the feathers tilt and separate to offer the minimum of resistance to the air.

Feathers on the upstroke

Feathers on the downstroke

During the downstroke they close, overlapping like roof tiles, to give the maximum of push.

Section of a bird's bone

A bird's bones, which are hollow and contain air, are particularly light and strong. Over half its weight is muscle.

Vaned feathers fall into two main groups: flight feathers which propel the bird, and tail feathers which steer its course. The flight feathers border the wings. The primaries are attached to bones which correspond to our hands, and the secondaries to bones which correspond to our arms. Covering the base of the flight feathers are the covert. The steering and stabilizing feathers, which form the tail, are attached to bones which correspond to the lower vertebrae.

Lesser wing coverts

Greater wing coverts

Primaries

Secondaries

Tail feathers

Magpie

Flapping Follies

Since the earliest times, people have looked at birds with admiration for their marvelous ability to fly. Soaring through the air, they seemed the freest of creatures.

Many brave inventors tried to build flapping devices, called ornithopters, which would imitate birds' wings, but none of them realized what enormous strength would be needed to propel them, or what skill to guide them. It was many years before the discovery of the secret of how to design aerodynamic wings.

The Italian artist and designer Leonardo da Vinci, for one, drew numerous sketches of ornithopters. Happily none of his ideas were ever really put into practice, for the pilot would surely have crashed.

Sketches by Leonardo da Vinci, about 1500

Later in life, Leonardo studied birds and made many sketches of them. Unfortunately, his drawings were not published until centuries later, and so could not advance aviation.

In 1678 a French locksmith named Besnier claimed that he had invented a pair of flapping paddles which he had used to cross rivers and fly over his neighbors' houses. More likely, he used them once and got a cold dunking for it!

In 1781 another Frenchman, Jean Pierre Blanchard, dreamed up this boat, which he hoped to paddle not through water but through air! Fortunately, he suspended his craft from a cord and tested it, and, doubtless disappointed with the results, took the idea no further. Four years later, however, he successfully crossed the Channel by hydrogen balloon.

In 1801 a French general named Resnier de Goué built and tested an ornithopter at the age of seventy-two. Lucky to survive the inevitable fall with nothing worse than a broken leg, he told the story until his death ten years later.

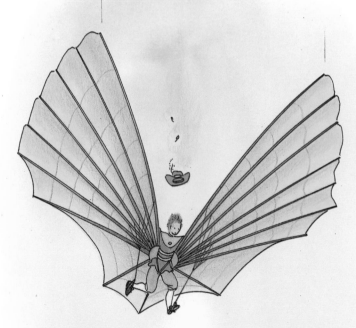

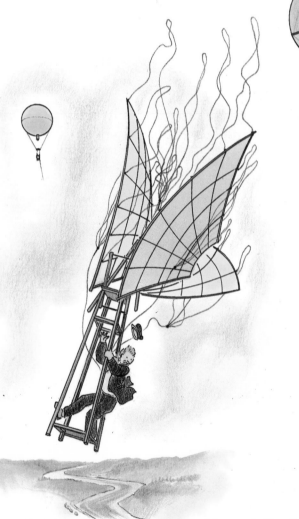

On July 9, 1874, a Belgian inventor, Vincent de Groof, attached his ornithopter to a balloon and was towed skyward over London. He cut the cord to begin his flight, and it was the last thing he ever did.

Searching for the Secret of Wings

The secret of wings lies in their shape. To be effective, they must cut swiftly through the air. The upper side of a wing is curved in such a way that the air passing over it has further to travel than the air below and is forced to go faster.

This spreads the particles more thinly. The pressure exerted on the wing from above is less than that exerted from below, so the air below the wing literally pushes it upward and keeps it in flight. In truth, wings perform a trick on the air, and the sight of them lifting the heaviest aircraft into the sky is magical.

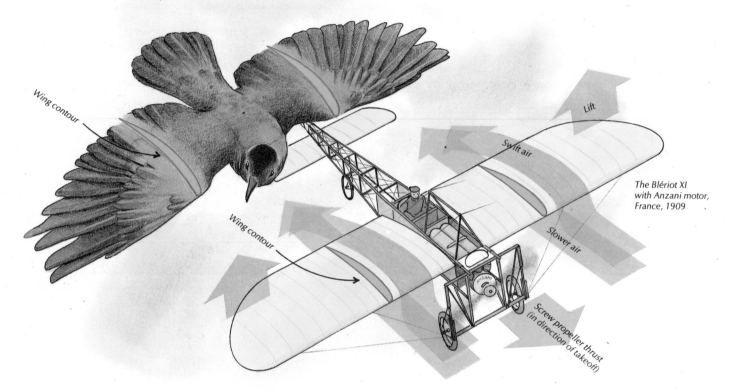

Wing contour

Wing contour

Lift

Swift air

Slower air

Screw propeller thrust (in direction of takeoff)

The Blériot XI with Anzani motor, France, 1909

Fast air

Lift is produced

Cut-off air

To test the secret of wings for yourself, take a sheet of thin, light paper. Hold it so that it is hanging downward, at about the level of your lower lip. Take a deep breath and blow strongly. The wind of your breath reduces the pressure on the outer surface . . . and the sheet begins to rise!

Between 1891 and 1896, after years of study and experiment, the German inventor Otto Lilienthal made a series of long hops and glides which excited the world. Photographs of them were published widely, and inspired others to try their hand at gliding, too. Lilienthal's love of gliding was to cost him his life.

The automobile was invented at the same time as Lilienthal was making his glides. Inside it was the gasoline engine: light but powerful, this was the missing element, enabling aircraft to take to the air at last.

Otto Lilienthal was a German inventor who studied the flight of birds very carefully and realized that the secret did not lie in the flapping of the wings but in their shape. He built several gliders, taking great care over them, and in 1891 propelled himself down the slope of a hill near Berlin and took off in the first successful glide.

The Birth of Powered Flight

With proper wings, it was possible to build a glider. But to build a powered aircraft, and fly like a bird, was a much larger problem! Birds have very strong muscles to operate their wings, and an airplane, similarly, needs a strong power-plant to propel it through the air.

The first practical aircraft engine, light yet powerful, was derived from the gasoline engine of the newly invented automobile. But to design a complete and practical aircraft from scratch took more than wings and a motor. It took genius. Fortunately the genius was at hand.

Otto Lilienthal

The Wright brothers were bicycle-builders from Dayton in Ohio. They first became interested in flying when they read an article about Lilienthal's glides in Germany. Like him, they understood that a controlled flight was the only successful one. They experimented with winged kites and gliders, and found that by changing the angle of the wingtips they could keep the craft steady in the wind and bank it from side to side. The technique was to become known as "wing-warping".

Wilbur and Orville Wright

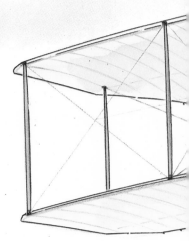

The Wright brothers made many glides on the windy beaches near Kitty Hawk in North Carolina.

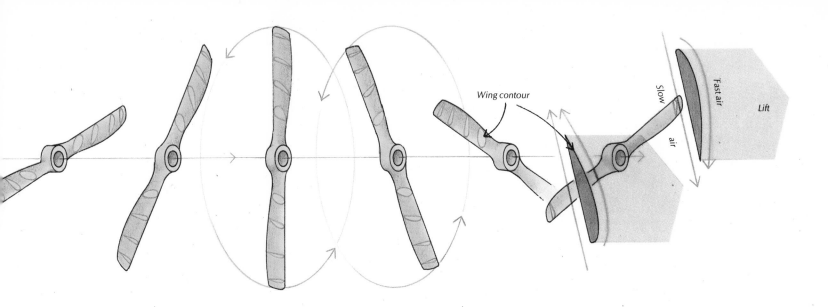

Wing contour

Slow air

Fast air

Lift

In the winter of 1903 the Wright brothers brought to their campsite a craft powered by two pusher propellers. They called their craft the *Flyer*, and took turns trying to fly it. On December 17, they launched it from a trolley running along a rail laid in the sand, into the wind. It was Orville who was aboard when the machine lifted off, dipped and rose, and landed about 120 feet (36 meters) away. They made three more flights, the longest being 852 feet (260 meters), on that historic day.

A wing will lift if air rushes swiftly over its upper surface. If you mount a wing on a peg and make it spin very fast, once again it should lift into the air. A propeller is essentially a pair of spinning wings, lifting themselves up into, and through, the air.

Flying

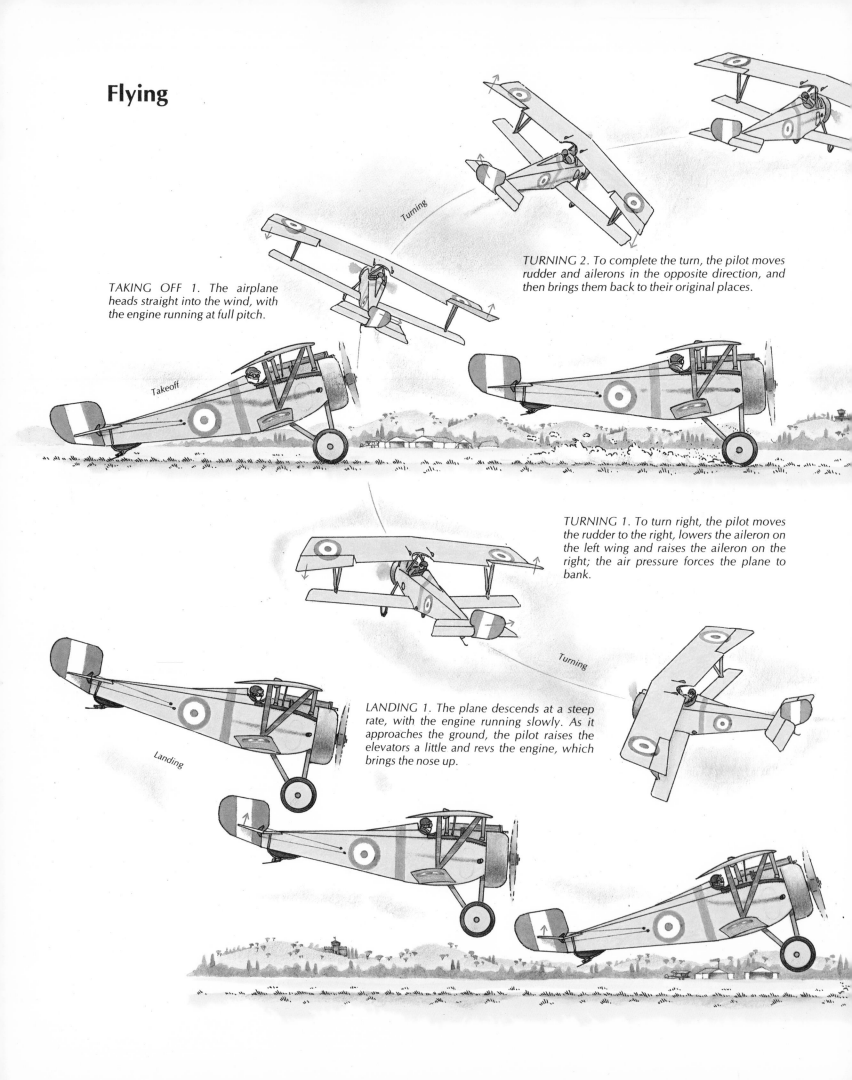

TAKING OFF 1. The airplane heads straight into the wind, with the engine running at full pitch.

Takeoff

Turning

TURNING 2. To complete the turn, the pilot moves rudder and ailerons in the opposite direction, and then brings them back to their original places.

TURNING 1. To turn right, the pilot moves the rudder to the right, lowers the aileron on the left wing and raises the aileron on the right; the air pressure forces the plane to bank.

Turning

LANDING 1. The plane descends at a steep rate, with the engine running slowly. As it approaches the ground, the pilot raises the elevators a little and revs the engine, which brings the nose up.

Landing

Of all the Earth's oceans, the Ocean of Air is perhaps the most difficult to sail! Any aircraft is constantly affected by turbulence, buffeting winds and abrupt changes of weather.

Every airplane is equipped with controls, and an experienced pilot can maneuver it with the agility of a bird. The three basic maneuvers are taking off, turning the plane, and landing.

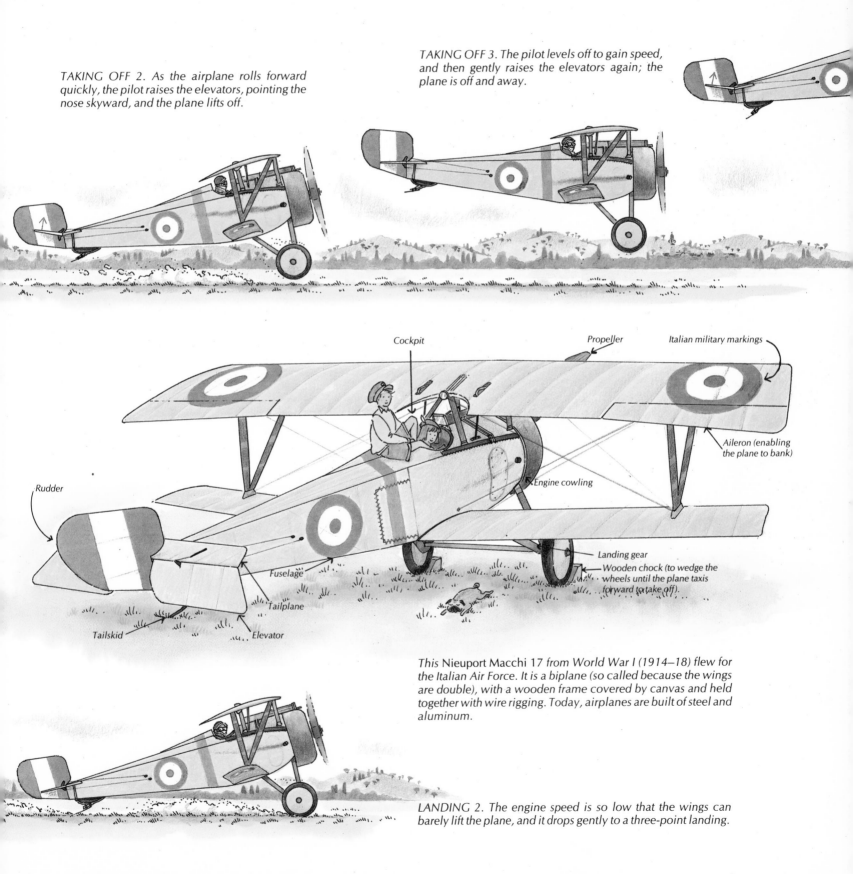

TAKING OFF 2. As the airplane rolls forward quickly, the pilot raises the elevators, pointing the nose skyward, and the plane lifts off.

TAKING OFF 3. The pilot levels off to gain speed, and then gently raises the elevators again; the plane is off and away.

Cockpit

Propeller

Italian military markings

Aileron (enabling the plane to bank)

Engine cowling

Rudder

Fuselage

Tailplane

Tailskid

Elevator

Landing gear

Wooden chock (to wedge the wheels until the plane taxis forward to take off).

This Nieuport Macchi 17 from World War I (1914–18) flew for the Italian Air Force. It is a biplane (so called because the wings are double), with a wooden frame covered by canvas and held together with wire rigging. Today, airplanes are built of steel and aluminum.

LANDING 2. The engine speed is so low that the wings can barely lift the plane, and it drops gently to a three-point landing.

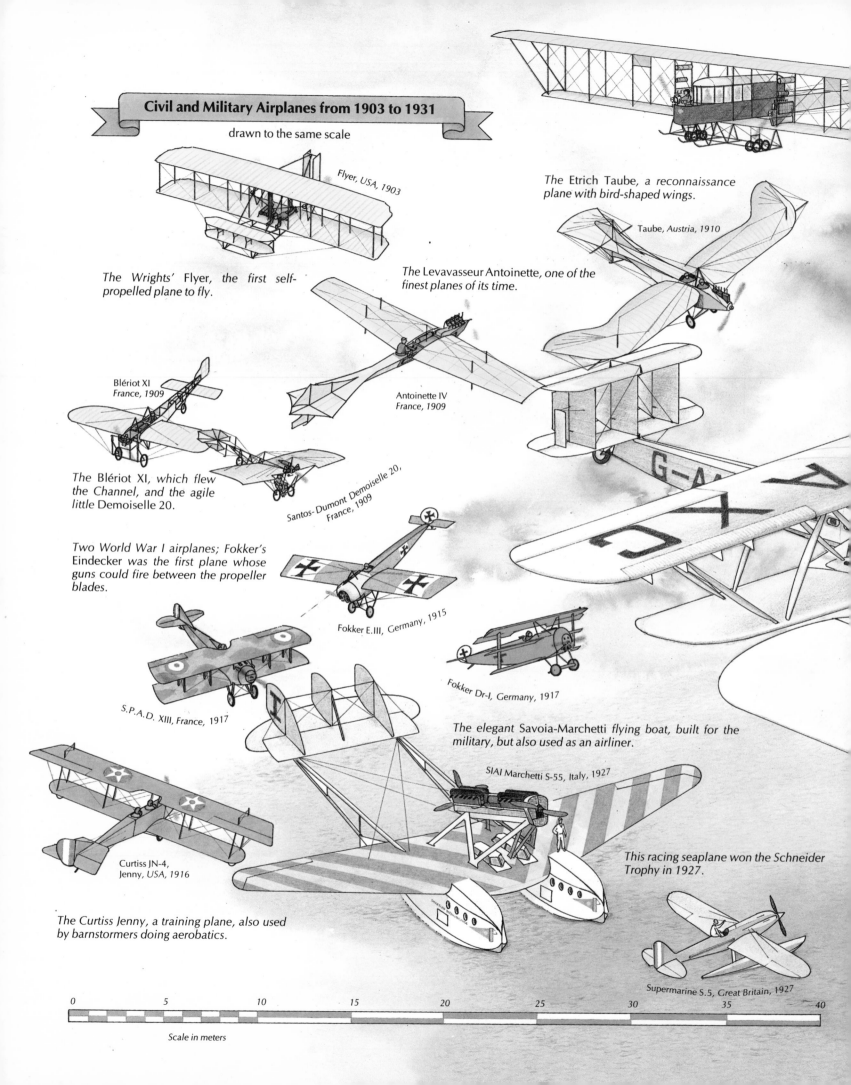

Civil and Military Airplanes from 1903 to 1931

drawn to the same scale

Flyer, USA, 1903

The Etrich Taube, *a reconnaissance plane with bird-shaped wings.*

Taube, Austria, 1910

The Wrights' Flyer, the first self-propelled plane to fly.

The Levavasseur Antoinette, one of the finest planes of its time.

Antoinette IV France, 1909

Blériot XI France, 1909

The Blériot XI, which flew the Channel, and the agile little Demoiselle 20.

Santos-Dumont Demoiselle 20, France, 1909

Two World War I airplanes; Fokker's Eindecker *was the first plane whose guns could fire between the propeller blades.*

Fokker E.III, Germany, 1915

Fokker Dr-I, Germany, 1917

S.P.A.D. XIII, France, 1917

The elegant Savoia-Marchetti flying boat, built for the military, but also used as an airliner.

SIAI Marchetti S-55, Italy, 1927

Curtiss JN-4, Jenny, USA, 1916

This racing seaplane won the Schneider Trophy in 1927.

The Curtiss Jenny, a training plane, also used by barnstormers doing aerobatics.

Supermarine S.5, Great Britain, 1927

| 0 | | 5 | | 10 | | 15 | | 20 | | 25 | | 30 | | 35 | | 40 |

Scale in meters

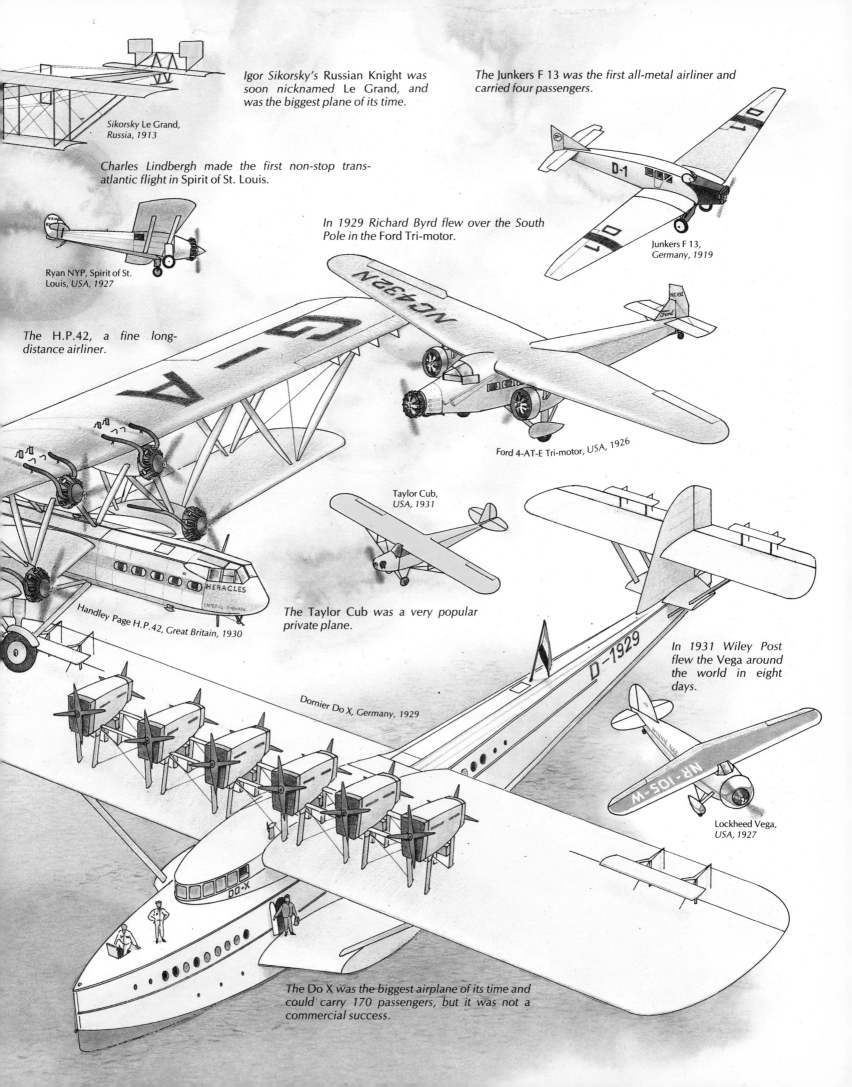

Igor Sikorsky's Russian Knight was soon nicknamed Le Grand, and was the biggest plane of its time.

Sikorsky Le Grand, Russia, 1913

The Junkers F 13 was the first all-metal airliner and carried four passengers.

Junkers F 13, Germany, 1919

Charles Lindbergh made the first non-stop trans-atlantic flight in Spirit of St. Louis.

Ryan NYP, Spirit of St. Louis, USA, 1927

In 1929 Richard Byrd flew over the South Pole in the Ford Tri-motor.

The H.P.42, a fine long-distance airliner.

Ford 4-AT-E Tri-motor, USA, 1926

Taylor Cub, USA, 1931

Handley Page H.P.42, Great Britain, 1930

The Taylor Cub was a very popular private plane.

In 1931 Wiley Post flew the Vega around the world in eight days.

Dornier Do X, Germany, 1929

Lockheed Vega, USA, 1927

The Do X was the biggest airplane of its time and could carry 170 passengers, but it was not a commercial success.

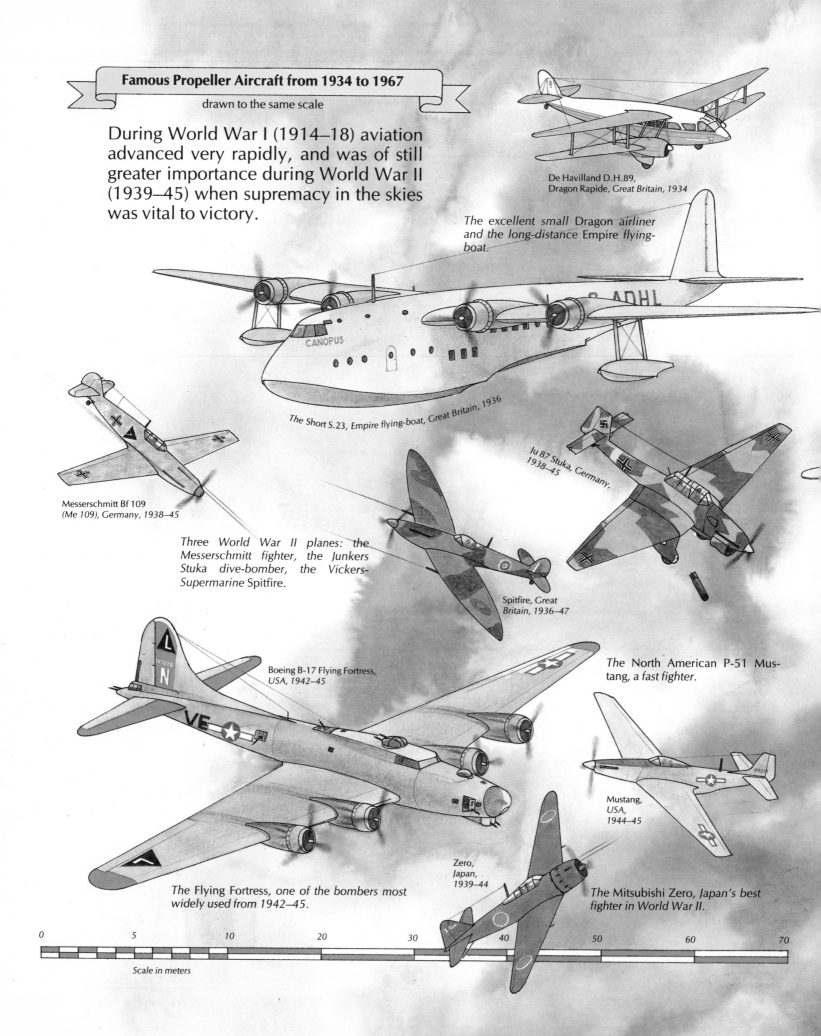

Famous Propeller Aircraft from 1934 to 1967

drawn to the same scale

During World War I (1914–18) aviation advanced very rapidly, and was of still greater importance during World War II (1939–45) when supremacy in the skies was vital to victory.

De Havilland D.H.89, Dragon Rapide, *Great Britain, 1934*

The excellent *small* Dragon *airliner and the long-distance* Empire *flying-boat.*

The Short S.23, Empire flying-boat, *Great Britain, 1936*

Messerschmitt Bf 109 (Me 109), *Germany, 1938–45*

Ju 87 Stuka, *Germany, 1938–45*

Three *World War II planes: the* Messerschmitt *fighter, the* Junkers Stuka *dive-bomber, the* Vickers-Supermarine Spitfire.

Spitfire, *Great Britain, 1936–47*

Boeing B-17 Flying Fortress, *USA, 1942–45*

The North American P-51 Mustang, *a fast fighter.*

Mustang, *USA, 1944–45*

Zero, *Japan, 1939–44*

The Flying Fortress, *one of the bombers most widely used from 1942–45.*

The Mitsubishi Zero, *Japan's best fighter in World War II.*

0   5   10   20   30   40   50   60   70

Scale in meters

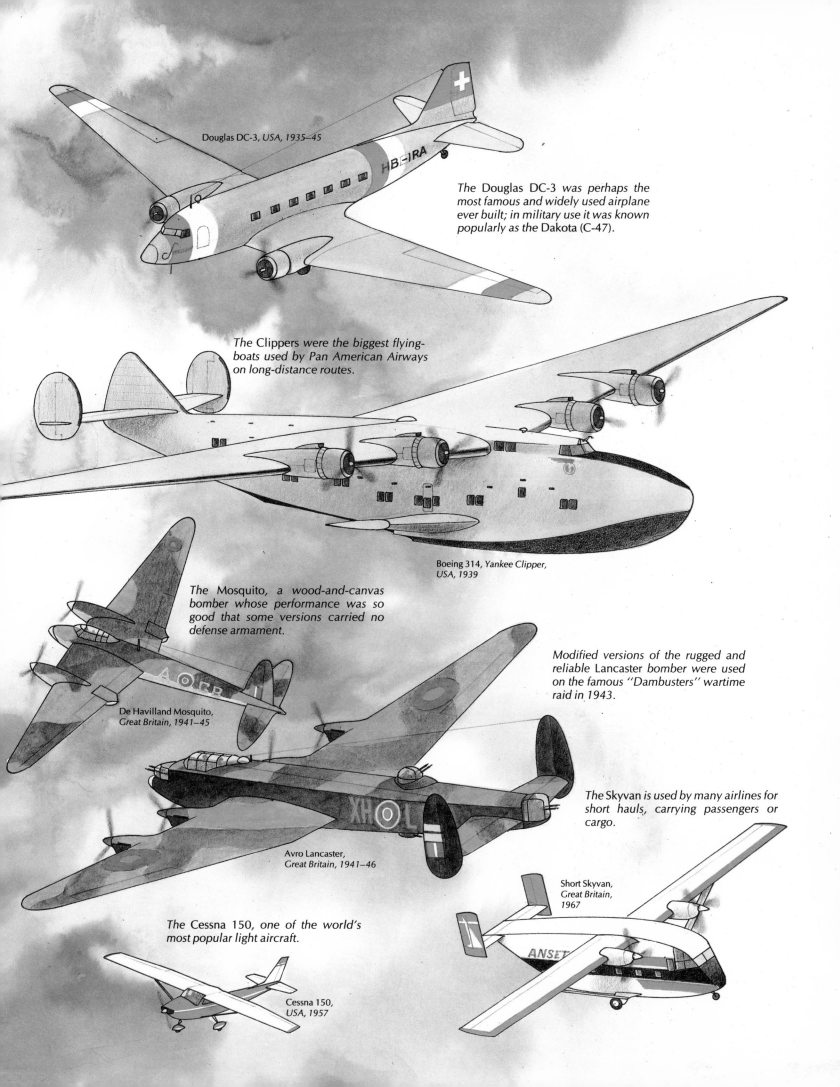

Douglas DC-3, *USA, 1935–45*

The Douglas DC-3 *was perhaps the most famous and widely used airplane ever built; in military use it was known popularly as the Dakota (C-47).*

The Clippers *were the biggest flying-boats used by Pan American Airways on long-distance routes.*

Boeing 314, Yankee Clipper, *USA, 1939*

The Mosquito, *a wood-and-canvas bomber whose performance was so good that some versions carried no defense armament.*

De Havilland Mosquito, *Great Britain, 1941–45*

Modified versions of the rugged and reliable Lancaster *bomber were used on the famous "Dambusters" wartime raid in 1943.*

Avro Lancaster, *Great Britain, 1941–46*

The Skyvan *is used by many airlines for short hauls, carrying passengers or cargo.*

Short Skyvan, *Great Britain, 1967*

The Cessna 150, *one of the world's most popular light aircraft.*

Cessna 150, *USA, 1957*

Winged seed-pod
spiraling gently
to the ground

Toy spinner

Drawing of a toy rotor
designed by George Cayley
in 1809

Helicopters

A helicopter has wings, too, but with a difference. They are active, spinning as a rotor above the craft, and generating their own lift. This makes a helicopter uniquely maneuverable. It can hover overhead, slide through the air in any direction, and take off from or land in the most inaccessible spots.

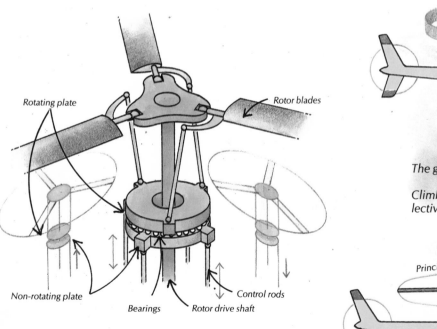

Rotating plate

Rotor blades

Non-rotating plate

Bearings   Rotor drive shaft

Control rods

The helicopter owes its maneuverability to its swashplate. Located below the rotor, and connected by rods to the controls, it can tilt the rotor disc to any angle, enabling the craft to slide in the desired direction. The upper plate spins with the rotor, the lower does not.

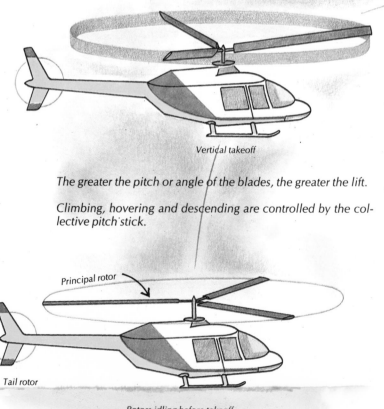

Vertical takeoff

The greater the pitch or angle of the blades, the greater the lift.

Climbing, hovering and descending are controlled by the collective pitch stick.

Principal rotor

Tail rotor

Rotors idling before takeoff

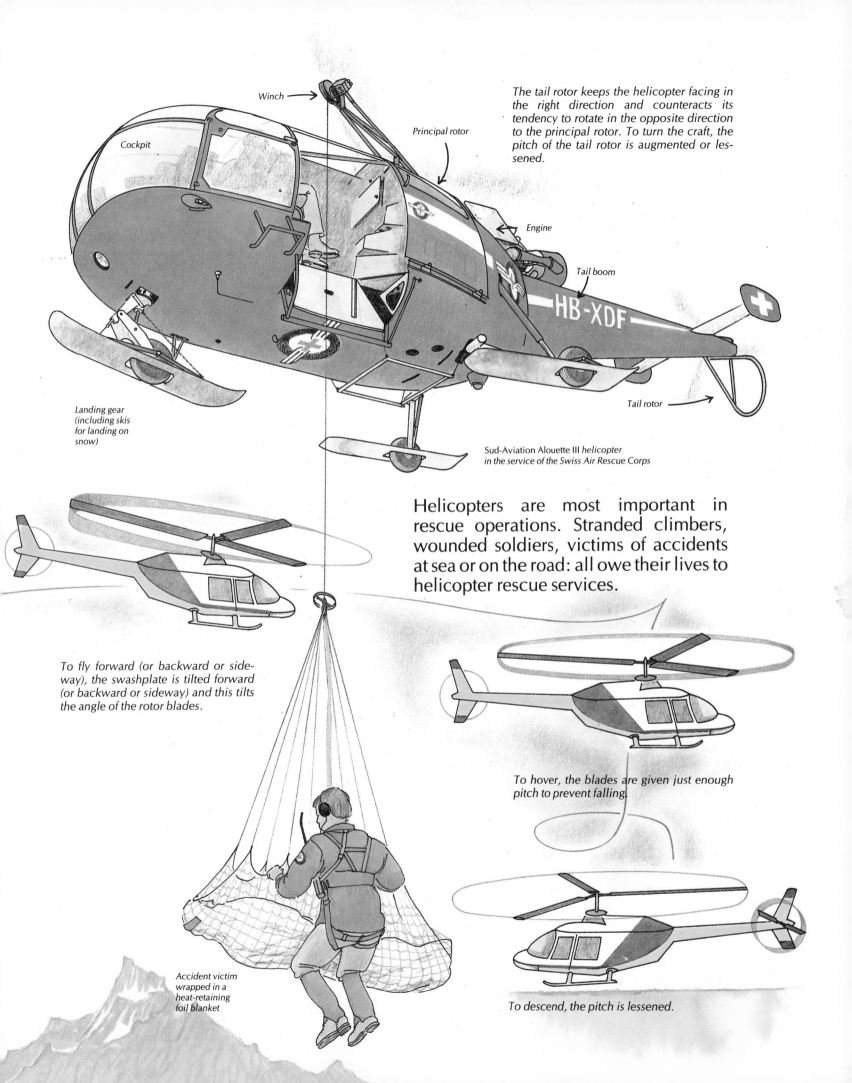

Winch

Cockpit

Principal rotor

The tail rotor keeps the helicopter facing in the right direction and counteracts its tendency to rotate in the opposite direction to the principal rotor. To turn the craft, the pitch of the tail rotor is augmented or lessened.

Engine

Tail boom

HB-XDF

Landing gear (including skis for landing on snow)

Tail rotor

Sud-Aviation Alouette III *helicopter in the service of the Swiss Air Rescue Corps*

Helicopters are most important in rescue operations. Stranded climbers, wounded soldiers, victims of accidents at sea or on the road: all owe their lives to helicopter rescue services.

To fly forward (or backward or sideway), the swashplate is tilted forward (or backward or sideway) and this tilts the angle of the rotor blades.

To hover, the blades are given just enough pitch to prevent falling.

Accident victim wrapped in a heat-retaining foil blanket

To descend, the pitch is lessened.

Jets

Not all aircraft have propellers or rotors. Most modern airplanes are jets. Jet engines work on a very simple principle: that every action causes an opposite reaction. Suppose you are stepping out of a row boat on to a jetty. As you push yourself forward from the boat to reach the jetty, the boat is moved backward (and you end up in the water!). Every action causes an opposite reaction, and the action and reaction are equal.

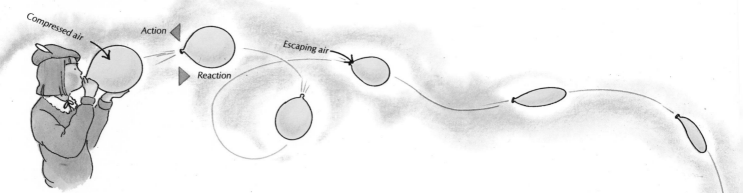

If you blow up a toy balloon and then let it go, the air escaping backward from the balloon (the action) pushes the balloon forward (the reaction). Jet engines work in just this way.

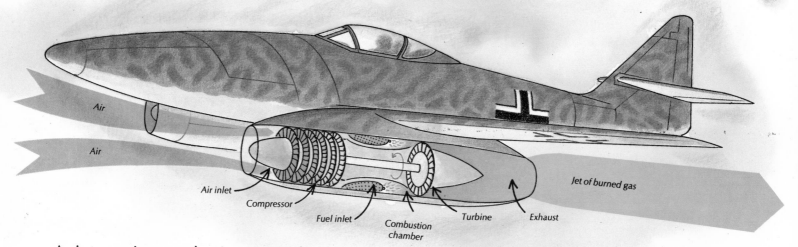

A jet engine sucks in air to be compressed by the turbine blades and ignited with the fuel in the combustion chamber. The backward rush of expanding air operates the turbine and roars through the exhaust, thrusting the jet forward.

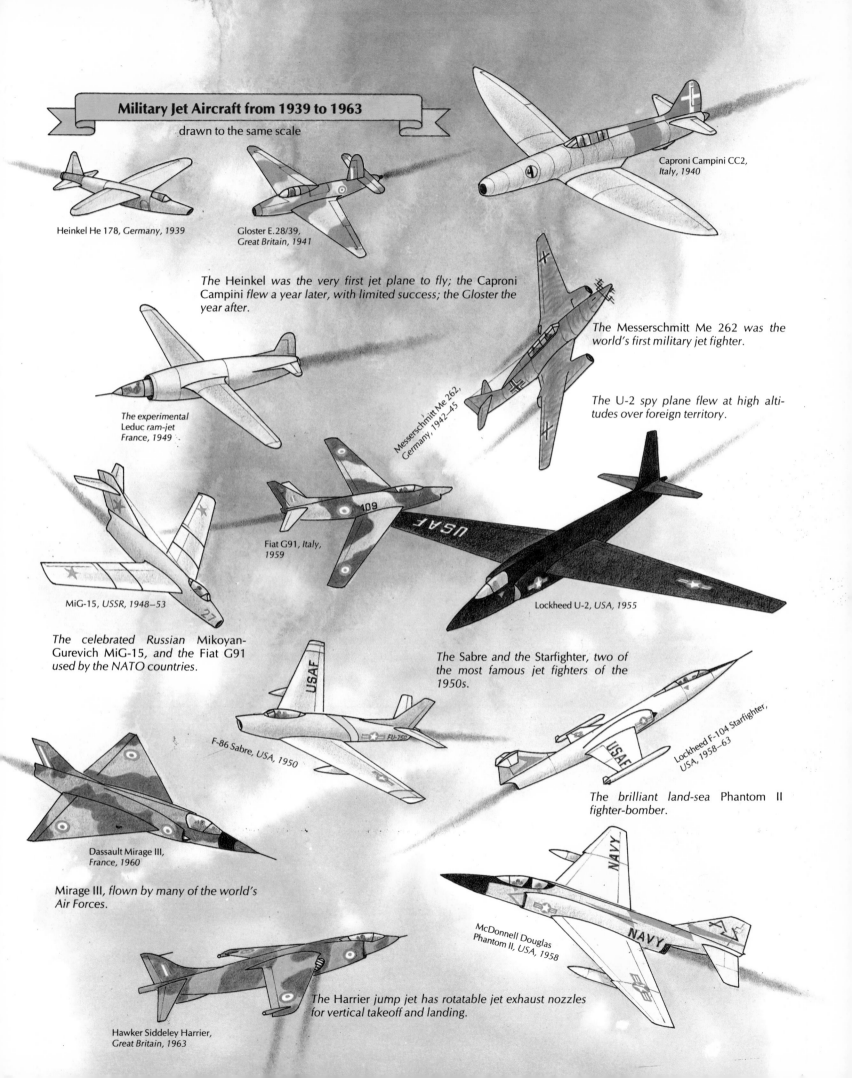

Military Jet Aircraft from 1939 to 1963
drawn to the same scale

Caproni Campini CC2,
Italy, 1940

Heinkel He 178, *Germany, 1939*

Gloster E.28/39,
Great Britain, 1941

The Heinkel *was the very first jet plane to fly; the* Caproni
Campini *flew a year later, with limited success; the* Gloster *the
year after.*

The Messerschmitt Me 262 *was the
world's first military jet fighter.*

The experimental
Leduc ram-jet
France, 1949

Messerschmitt Me 262,
Germany, 1942–45

The U-2 *spy plane flew at high altitudes over foreign territory.*

Fiat G91, *Italy,
1959*

Lockheed U-2, *USA, 1955*

MiG-15, *USSR, 1948–53*

The celebrated Russian Mikoyan-
Gurevich MiG-15, *and the* Fiat G91
used by the NATO countries.

The Sabre *and the* Starfighter, *two of
the most famous jet fighters of the
1950s.*

F-86 Sabre, *USA, 1950*

Lockheed F-104 Starfighter,
USA, 1958–63

The brilliant land-sea Phantom II
fighter-bomber.

Dassault Mirage III,
France, 1960

Mirage III, *flown by many of the world's
Air Forces.*

McDonnell Douglas
Phantom II, *USA, 1958*

Hawker Siddeley Harrier,
Great Britain, 1963

The Harrier *jump jet has rotatable jet exhaust nozzles
for vertical takeoff and landing.*

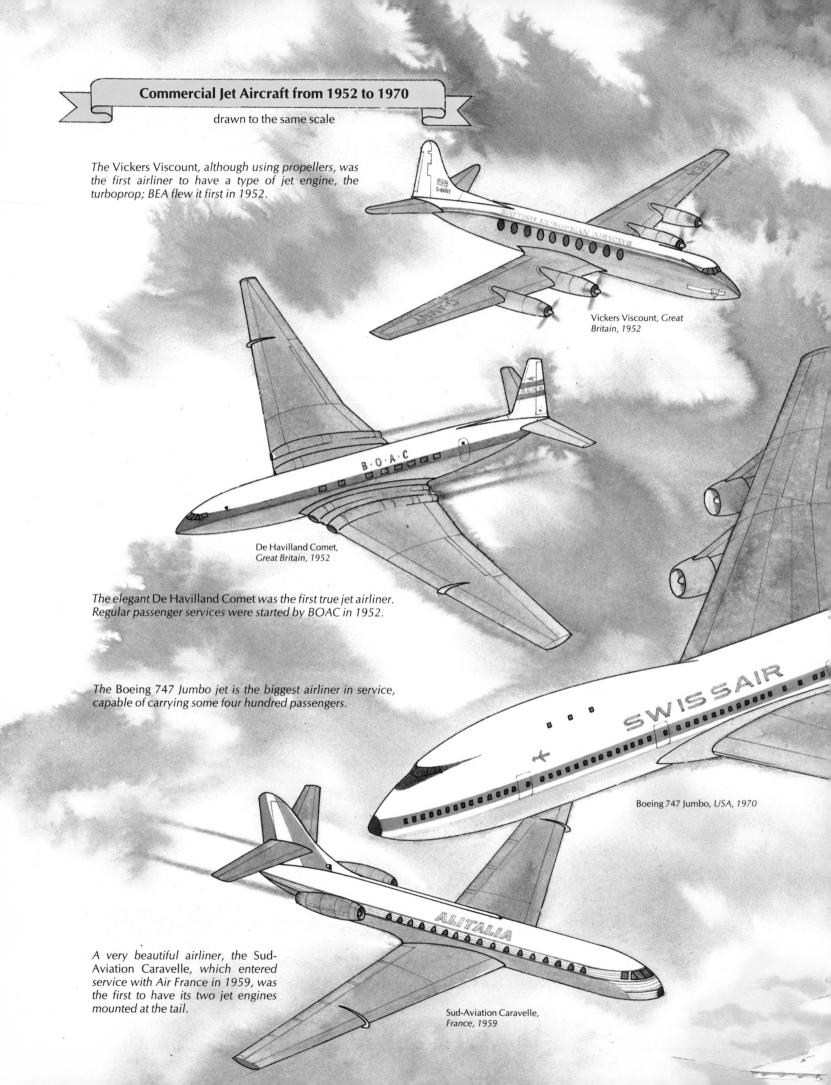

Commercial Jet Aircraft from 1952 to 1970

drawn to the same scale

The Vickers Viscount, although using propellers, was the first airliner to have a type of jet engine, the turboprop; BEA flew it first in 1952.

Vickers Viscount, *Great Britain, 1952*

De Havilland Comet, *Great Britain, 1952*

The elegant De Havilland Comet *was the first true jet airliner. Regular passenger services were started by BOAC in 1952.*

The Boeing 747 Jumbo jet is the biggest airliner in service, capable of carrying some four hundred passengers.

Boeing 747 Jumbo, *USA, 1970*

A very beautiful airliner, the Sud-Aviation Caravelle, *which entered service with Air France in 1959, was the first to have its two jet engines mounted at the tail.*

Sud-Aviation Caravelle, *France, 1959*

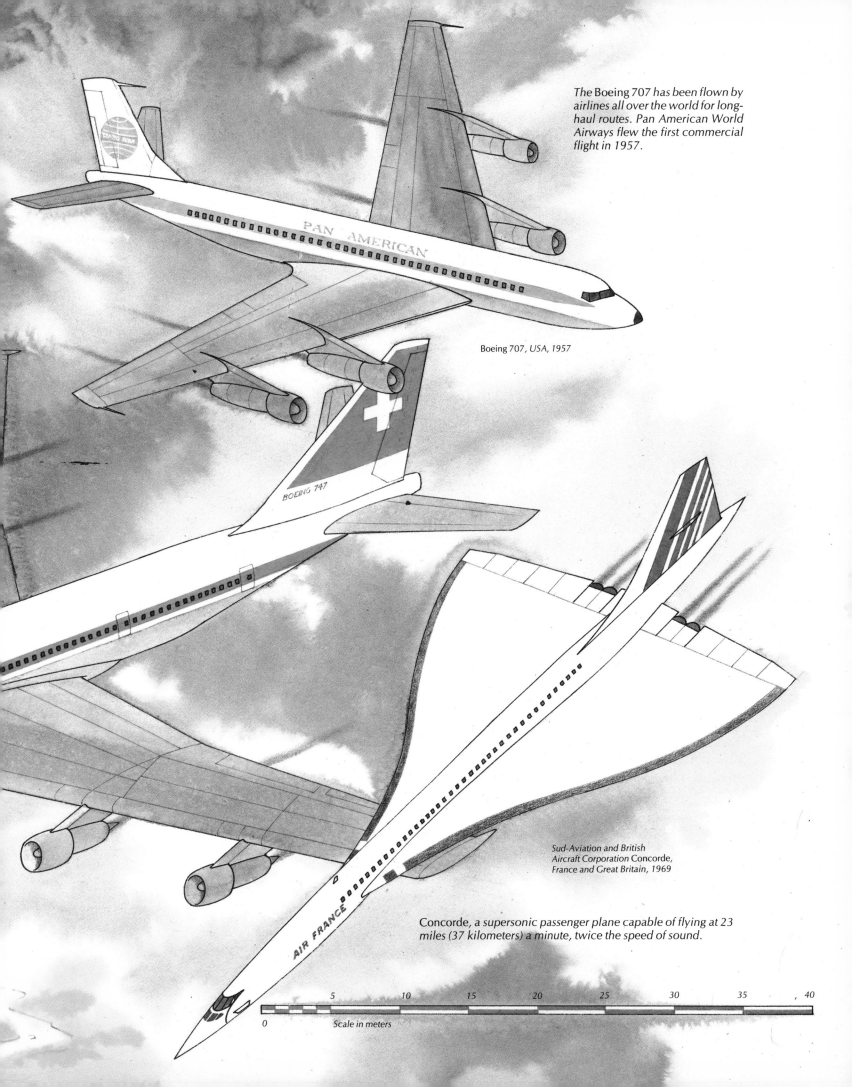

The Boeing 707 has been flown by airlines all over the world for long-haul routes. Pan American World Airways flew the first commercial flight in 1957.

Boeing 707, *USA, 1957*

Sud-Aviation and British Aircraft Corporation Concorde, France and Great Britain, 1969

Concorde, a supersonic passenger plane capable of flying at 23 miles (37 kilometers) a minute, twice the speed of sound.

0   5   10   15   20   25   30   35   40
Scale in meters

How Grandad Used to Fly . . .

Air travel has changed tremendously since the first airplanes took to the air, at the start of the century. The first fliers used a flat grassy field for takeoff and landing. They didn't go too far from home, and they flew in fair weather so that they could spot landmarks below and check their position by a road map. But at night, or over the sea, or in fog, pilots needed a navigation system. Dead reckoning was the simplest means of finding the way.

The Etrich Taube, 1910

0   10   20   30   40   50   60   70   80   90   100   110   120   130   140 Miles

Lindbergh's Spirit of St. Louis 1927

Compass

Map

If you know your position at, say, 8 o'clock, and fly due east at 140 miles per hour, keeping to a compass heading of 90°, at 9 o'clock you should be 140 miles due east of your original position; and so you can plot a course from point to point. The system isn't foolproof as it doesn't allow for cross-winds pushing you off course, but in 1927 Lindbergh found his way across the Atlantic by dead reckoning alone.

The invention of radio was an enormous help; with the aid of a loop aerial, you could pick up radio beams and vary their intensity.

By lining up the transmitter with the angle of the aerial, you knew the line along which the plane was flying, and by lining up a second transmitter you had your exact position.

Loop aerial

Radio operator

SIAI Marchetti S.M.

Radio transmitter

This is an airport fifty years ago. The airplane is a Fokker F-VIIa monoplane of 1931, which carried between eight and ten passengers, cruised at 100–15 mph (165–85 kmh) and could fly about 500 miles (800 kilometers) without refueling. The cabin was tiny, with lightweight wicker chairs, and big windows gave a good view of the ground, which was never very far below. A flight attendant served light refreshments and gave you chewing gum or barley sugar to keep your ears from popping.

The airport was a flat grassy field, which was large enough for airplanes to take off or land into the wind, from whichever direction it was blowing. The windsock showed the wind's direction. The field was lined with hangars, where the aircraft were stored and repaired. The airport kept in touch with the pilots thanks to radio.

. . . and a Typical Flight Today

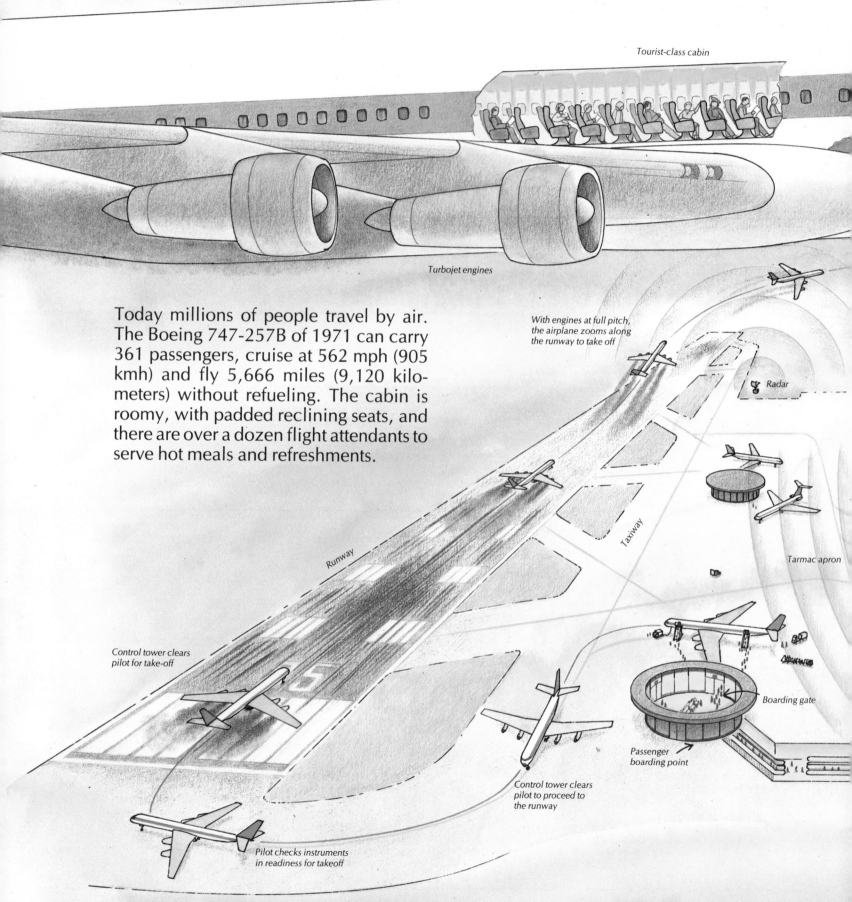

Boeing 747 *Jumbo jet*

Tourist-class cabin

Turbojet engines

Today millions of people travel by air. The Boeing 747-257B of 1971 can carry 361 passengers, cruise at 562 mph (905 kmh) and fly 5,666 miles (9,120 kilometers) without refueling. The cabin is roomy, with padded reclining seats, and there are over a dozen flight attendants to serve hot meals and refreshments.

With engines at full pitch, the airplane zooms along the runway to take off

Radar

Taxiway

Tarmac apron

Runway

Control tower clears pilot for take-off

Boarding gate

Passenger boarding point

Control tower clears pilot to proceed to the runway

Pilot checks instruments in readiness for takeoff

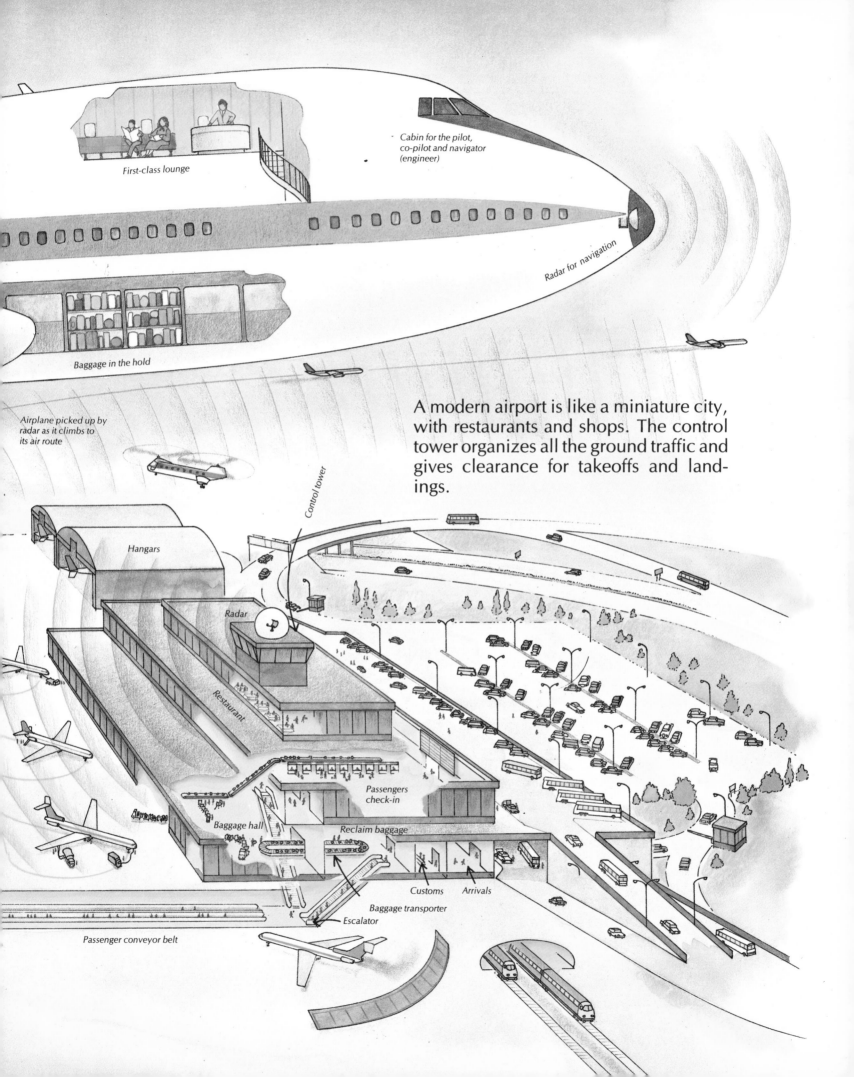

First-class lounge

Cabin for the pilot,
co-pilot and navigator
(engineer)

Radar for navigation

Baggage in the hold

Airplane picked up by
radar as it climbs to
its air route

A modern airport is like a miniature city,
with restaurants and shops. The control
tower organizes all the ground traffic and
gives clearance for takeoffs and land-
ings.

Control tower

Hangars

Radar

Restaurant

Passengers
check-in

Baggage hall

Reclaim baggage

Customs

Arrivals

Baggage transporter

Escalator

Passenger conveyor belt

Air routes

Radar station

Radio transmitter

Radio link

Air traffic controllers

Radio beacon
marking air routes

Air traffic
control center

The Highways of the Sky

With so many airplanes in the sky today, their greatest problem is to keep out of each other's way. They travel along air routes, or corridors, in the sky, each route being about 11 miles (18 kilometers) wide and 1,000 feet (300 meters) above or below any other, marked by radio beacons at the intersections. The Earth is divided up into regions under air traffic control centers, and every airplane, wherever in the world it may be, is in constant touch with an air traffic controller, who uses radar to track the aircraft overhead, tells the pilots when to change course, and keeps the planes a safe distance apart. Many airports use Instrument Landing System (ILS) transmitters to feed the correct approach path to the instruments in the cockpit, so that landing is automated. Flying today is done largely from the ground.

Once safely down, the pilot reverses the thrust of his jet engines, which helps to brake the airplane, and the control tower guides him to the point where the passengers will disembark.

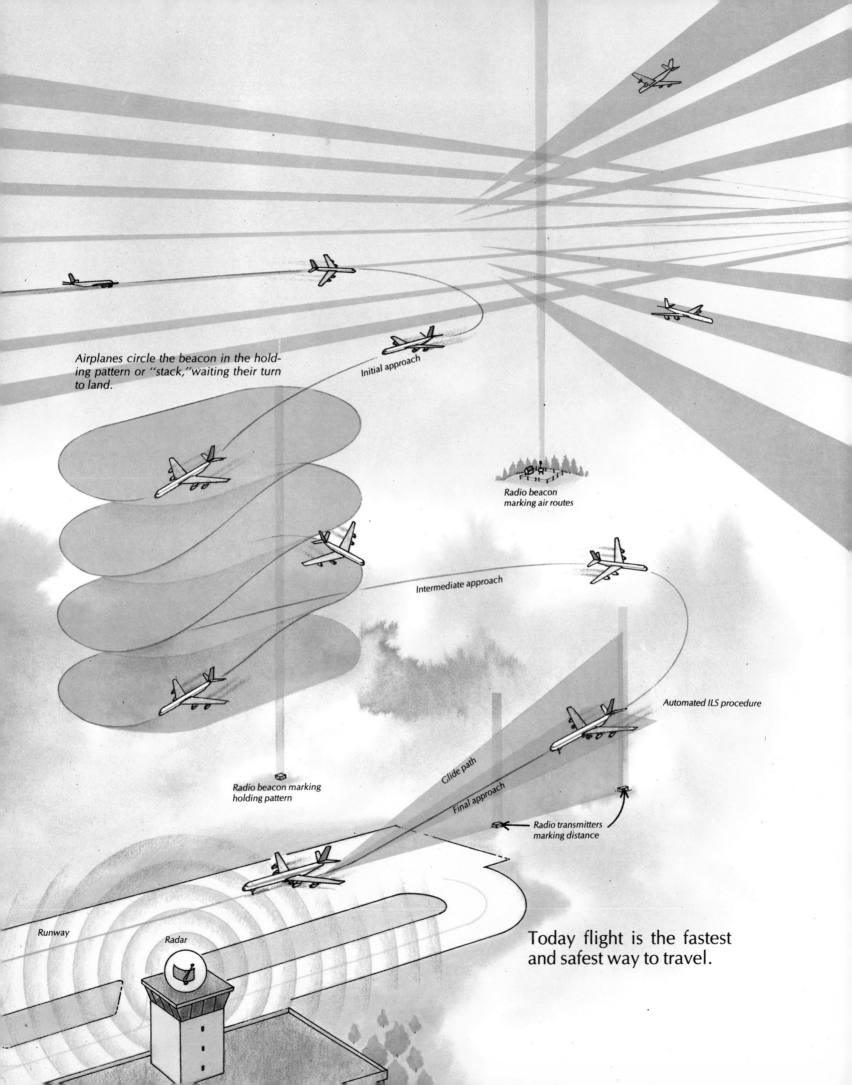

Airplanes circle the beacon in the holding pattern or "stack," waiting their turn to land.

Initial approach

Radio beacon
marking air routes

Intermediate approach

Radio beacon marking
holding pattern

Automated ILS procedure

Glide path

Final approach

Radio transmitters
marking distance

Runway

Radar

Today flight is the fastest
and safest way to travel.